Amazing Grace! Lord Jesus Lives!

New Britain

Carol Greene

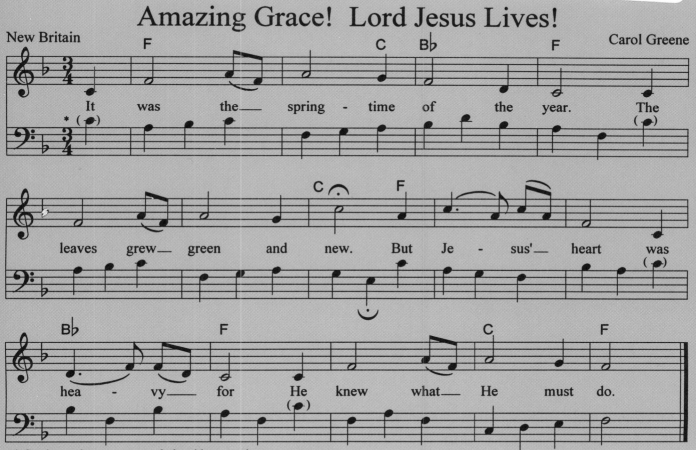

It was the spring-time of the year. The leaves grew green and new. But Jesus' heart was hea-vy for He knew what He must do.

* Can be used as a countermelody, either as written or up an octave

CE
Gre

Published by Concordia Publishing House
3558 S. Jefferson Avenue, St. Louis, MO 63118-3968
Manufactured in the United States of America

2 3 4 5 6 7 8 9 10   07 06 05 04 03 02 01 00 99 98

Amazing Grace!
Lord Jesus Lives!

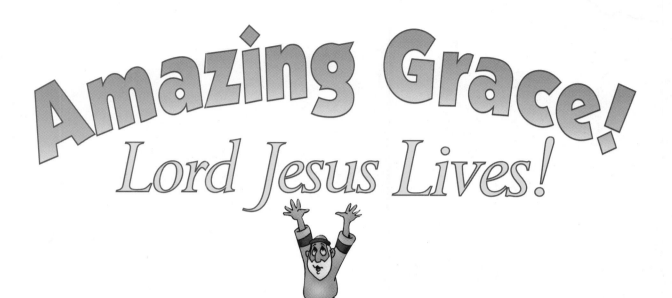

Carol Greene
Illustrated by Christopher Gray

*The text of this book may be sung to the
tune of "Amazing Grace."*

SAINT LOUIS

*I*t was the springtime of the year.
The leaves grew green and new.
But Jesus' heart was heavy, for
He knew what He must do.

So Jesus rode a donkey to
Jerusalem one day,
While cheering people threw their cloaks
And palms along His way.

"Hosanna to the Son of God!"
They shouted as He passed.
But Jesus knew their cheers of praise
Would change to jeers at last.

They nailed Lord Jesus to a cross
And left Him there to die.
The whole earth shook, the rocks split wide,
And darkness filled the sky.

"I put My spirit in Your hands,
My Father," Jesus cried.
And then the Lord who loved the world
Bowed down His head and died.

Some women stood and watched it all.
They would not run away.
They made up spices and perfumes
For after Sabbath day.

Then very early Easter morn,
They hurried to the tomb.
But Jesus wasn't lying there.
They found an empty room.

What can this mean? the women thought.
And wondered there and feared.
Then men in clothes like lightning all
At once to them appeared.

"He told you this would happen when
He was with you before:
How He must suffer for our sin.
But He is dead no more."

You see, God's promise had been kept
By God's beloved Son.
He died and rose that all might live,
Forgiven, every one.